DEB DUNCAN & TODD DUNCAN

Building High Ratings and High Trust in the Digital Age

simple truths

small books. BIG IMPACT.

Photo Credits
Cover: front, Yganko/Shutterstock, zaniman/Shutterstock
Internals: page 3, Yganko/Shutterstock, zaniman/Shutterstock; page 8, zaniman/Shutterstock; pages 10, 15, 16, 27, 34, 41, 46, 56–57, 63, 68, 78, 90, 93, 98, 105, 107, 108, 126, 133, 141, 146, 151, VectorState

Published by Simple Truths, an imprint of Sourcebooks, Inc.
P.O. Box 4410, Naperville, Illinois 60567-4410
(630) 961-3900
Fax: (630) 961-2168
www.sourcebooks.com

Printed and bound in China.
QL 10 9 8 7 6 5 4 3 2 1

CONTENTS

THE FUTURE OF SELLING

⭐ ⭐ ⭐ ⭐ ⭐

Chapter 1

> *Great companies start because the founders want to change the world...not make a fast buck.*
>
> — GUY KAWASAKI

One thing is for certain: the ratings race is on, and how a company's brand and service performs in the mind of the consumer is more important than ever. That's why a doctor texts his patient's mobile phone for a review while they are still in the office. That's why the hairstylist sends an email within an hour of the client leaving with a happy face or a sad face to determine the client's level of satisfaction. That's why Fandango asks a customer to rate the movie. That's why Uber asks you to rate the ride. That's why Nike wants you to rate the experience one day after your product arrives. Why? Because ratings matter and it's driving brand success and loyalty!

Technology and social media are revolutionizing business today. Those companies that understand how to balance technology with connection and trust will make the most money and get the highest ratings in the future, period.

For example, when Todd ran into an old buddy who had lost a lot of weight, Deb asked how he did it. It turns out that both the buddy and his wife had done the same weight-loss program, months apart, with impressive results.

The next day, Deb, who was interested in slimming down, checked the company's website and immediately a **big** promise popped up: lose twenty pounds in forty days. It seemed too good to be true, so after a bit of reading, she closed the link.

A few days later, a single question haunted her: "What if the promise is true?"

She researched a few top competitors' websites, but not a single one made a bold promise or had any kind of impressive, ballsy guarantee. Her conclusion: either the first company had great confidence in its results or it was a scam.

She dug deeper and tried to find some dirt from unhappy customers or claims the company made bogus promises. Surprisingly, she found a landslide of glowing reviews and 5-Star ratings of positive experiences.

A nicely produced, lengthy video, which explained the science and technology of the program, was prominent on the website. It did a magnificent job of overcoming objections and selling their brand philosophy. There was also a remarkable number of "V-Monials," or video testimonials, that she watched until her inner critic was satisfied.

The company has a ticking clock on the guarantee—results will be attained within forty days. There is no mention of price without a consultation at a local branch. The plot thickened.

The website also included a sales closer right before the Sign Up Now button for an appointment—an impressive checklist comparing their program against three of the top weight-loss programs.

Deb signed up online for the first available appointment to gather more information and the price. This company now has an *extremely eager potential client* for a big-ticket purchase, even before she's spoken or interacted with an actual person.

The day before the appointment, Deb received a phone call to confirm the time. That same day a confirmation email arrived. The morning of the appointment she received a text message with the appointment details. That's three confirmations using three different platforms of technology. Genius!

This company understands that depending on the generation of the client, people feel comfortable, and ultimately trustful, of different forms of technology.

Deb arrived at the office and a friendly receptionist asked her to watch a thirty-minute video that explained the steps and science of their program in greater detail, eliminating a large amount of questions and objections. At this point, she was all but sold, but she didn't know the price and hadn't spoken to a single salesperson.

In the next few steps of the sales process, each person Deb met had lost weight on the program—living testimonials to how awesome this system was. At this point, she was impressed enough, and with the protection of their guarantee and high ratings, she figured the worst that could happen was that she lost twenty pounds. The risk felt like it had been eliminated.

It was a brilliantly crafted program that did a masterful job of integrating trust, connection, and technology. They created accountability every morning by using an automated, interactive texting program. Deb texted her daily progress, which was monitored by a doctor—an approach that's both high touch and high trust. She was also given the doctor's and a weight-loss counselor's cell phone numbers that she could call or text—high trust.

By the fortieth day, Deb had not reached the guaranteed weight loss promised. The doctor reviewed her chart and said, "I gave you my word, and I'm a man of my word." He offered her the option of continuing on the program and extending it for an additional twenty days for free. That's a 50 percent extension at no cost—a high-trust move.

When you have something amazing to sell and can craft a well-choreographed customer experience using the latest technology, it's a win-win for your bottom line. Deb lost thirty pounds, and gave the company a 5-Star rating, saying it was the single best weight-loss program she had ever experienced.

5 THINGS EVERY BUSINESS NEEDS TO DO TO EARN 5 STARS IN THE DIGITAL MARKET

1. Acquire new customers.
2. Optimize that customer's purchase and service experience.
3. Retain and cultivate that customer for repeat business.
4. Increase the value of that customer by letting him or her attract new customers.
5. Repeat all the above!

LOW TRUST, HIGH TECH

The majority of companies still haven't fully figured out how to integrate trust and tech. In the process, they turn away scores of customers that could have ended up being 5-Star customers for life.

Recently, we were traveling and came across a full-page ad in a magazine. The headline read "Your Invitation to Try Better Snacks by Mail." Underneath it was another headline in huge font, "FREE BOX," followed by a cool picture of the gift you would receive.

The ad listed four steps in a very simple display of picture instructions. First, visit their website. Second, enter your information and the promo code. Third, identify the snacks you like. Fourth, look for your free box in the mail.

We went online, but apparently they left one step out of their ad. After giving them our data, including our email address and shipping address, a pop-up asked for our credit card information. This was *never* mentioned in the ad. We don't subscribe just to cancel and get a free gift. In our minds, this was a colossal breakdown of trust. Now, we are getting harassed with emails about signing up and the bottom line is that the company has lost our trust.

A company needs to acquire customers to deliver their goods, but what they don't want is thousands of customers who will remember their negative experience forever as collateral damage. This wasn't close to *5 Stars!*

HIGH TRUST, HIGH TECH

In-N-Out Burger is great at using technology and building trust. The company has an 800 number that anyone can call, and a friendly operator will get the customer's current location and give them directions to the closest In-N-Out location. Genius!

We have some friends that love In-N-Out Burger. They were on a road trip, stopped at a location for lunch, and for the first time ever were disappointed with the hamburgers. The meat was a little grisly.

As the couple drove away, they decided to call the 800 number

and let the operator know they were disappointed with their hamburgers. The operator apologized, said she'd contact that location's manager about the issue, requested the couple's address and cell phone number, and asked how much their meal was. They had spent twelve dollars. Two days later, the mail arrived with a note apologizing and inviting them back to In-N-Out with a thirty-dollar gift card, more than twice the amount of their previous purchase.

A few months later, the couple was driving by the same location and decided to stop and use their gift card. They ate lunch, got in their car, and were driving down the road when the husband's cell phone rang. It was the In-N-Out operator. She greeted them and said, "I see you returned to the same location and I was calling to see if you were happy with your burgers. I wanted to make sure they were not grisly this time."

In-N-Out did a spectacular job using technology to save a customer. They had the gift card linked to the couple's history and used a follow-up strategy with a live person who cared. They rebuilt trust and exceeded expectations! And the couple has continued to share their story with family and friends. This is 5 Stars!

WELCOME TO THE FUTURE

Every second, there are 2,472,160 emails sent, 118,294 YouTube videos viewed, 53,208 Google searches, 2,050 Skype calls made, 1,481 Tumblr posts uploaded, 487 Instagram photos published, and 7,135 tweets sent.

In the seconds it took you to read the above paragraph, all of those numbers increased by ten.

We are in the infancy of the technology revolution, and in the future, the speed and impact of a consumer's ability to positively or negatively influence others will increase exponentially. But, paradoxically, while high tech has increased our ability to communicate, it has decreased the amount of connection a customer feels with the companies he or she interacts with.

In business today, everyone in the company is in a high-stakes game to sell. Someone will get the customer! Someone will get the sale! The question is *who*.

This is where our journey begins—the future of selling. It's a world where high trust is more important than ever and is the catalyst for influence, retention, and referrals. It's a world where high tech can be a strategic advantage, helping to build digital fences of value around your client. This is the alchemy of 5 Stars.

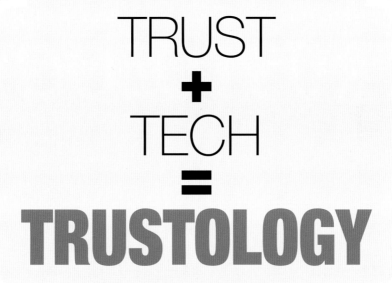

TRUST
+
TECH
=
TRUSTOLOGY

TRUSTOLOGY

★ ★ ★ ★ ★

Chapter 2

> *Trust is the glue of life. It's the most essential ingredient in effective communication. It's the foundational principle that holds all relationships—marriages, families, and organizations of every kind—together.*
>
> — STEPHEN R. COVEY

Trust is the new black. We mean that literally. Trust equals revenue. Trust equals profits. The most important currency in business is **trust**. It makes the bottom line happen and happen big. Without it, companies fight a continual uphill battle in winning and keeping customers. With it, those same companies win positive 5-Star ratings and reviews, which, in the digitally driven, social-media world, turn today's consumers into the most important influencers a brand can have. How important? Sixty-three percent of consumers say they are more likely to purchase in a high-trust environment. When those trust efforts are supported with technology, you have *trustology*. Trustology is a science. It's important that trust and tech are not seen as independent but rather interdependent. And when they come together, it's magic!

To leverage trustology, your customers need to believe and experience three things about your company:

1. You have their best interests at heart.
2. You are capable of delivering on your promises.
3. You and your product make them happier.

TRUSTOLOGY TRUTHS

The lower the trust, the lower the connection with a customer. This leads to fewer transactions and a higher acquisition cost for new clients.

According to a survey by the Harris Poll, 42 percent of consumers do not believe that companies that represent the top twenty industries are trustworthy.

According to another survey by PricewaterhouseCoopers, 62 percent of consumers trust brands less today than in the past.

Trustology is essential for any business to survive in today's world. If trust is not a priority in your business, you are behind the curve no matter how revolutionary or cool your product, service, or sales pitch is.

Trustology is the catalyst for performance. It's your competitive advantage—the reason people buy, come back, and tell their friends and colleagues about you, your product, and your service. Users of the top fifteen social media sites now number over 7.1 billion. These are not users, really. They are influencers. Add it all up and you have as many potential impressions daily as there are people on the planet.

Leading customer-intelligence firm Market Force found that more than 80 percent of online consumers reported friends' social media posts as moderately to highly influential on their purchase decisions, and 60 percent of them said they gather insights on companies, brands, and products from their friends' social media posts. Moreover, a Nielsen study showed that 92 percent of consumers around the world say they place the highest trust in *earned advertising*, such as recommendations from friends and family.

The most important purpose for your brand and your team is to create the highest trust possible 100 percent of the time with every customer served, period. This earns you 5 Stars.

> *Building, accelerating, and growing trust is the number one opportunity in business today.*
>
> — DEB DUNCAN

TAKING FLIGHT—HOW ONE BRAND EARNED 5 STARS

We were working on the island of Kauai, and we had a single day off that we could play and explore. The day before, a friend of ours had taken a helicopter tour with his wife and four kids. He was really impressed with the company and their exceptional customer service and suggested if we wanted to go for a ride that we use the same company—Blue Hawaiian Helicopters.

They have live reviews on their website with dozens of 5-Star recommendations from happy customers that were written that very same day. We also found an equally impressive number of reviews from the day before, and the day before, and so on. In their pursuit of trustology, Blue Hawaiian masterfully incorporated technology as a competitive advantage.

Their competitors' sites also had reviews, but you had to go looking for them and most were from previous years or had no date posted.

Blue Hawaiian's competitors may be equally impressive companies—or even superior companies with superior service and experience—but in this digital age, the vast majority of potential customers will make a decision about a company after visiting and comparing websites.

Blue Hawaiian Helicopters did three things brilliantly:

1. **Asked for reviews**

   The helicopter pilot asked the six people in the cockpit for a review before the helicopter landed. (The company has four helicopters flying every hour, so that's twenty-four possible reviews per hour.)

2. **Made it supereasy for clients to post reviews**

   When the flight was done, everyone had to pass through the Blue Hawaiian lobby and a retail space where people could buy hats, shirts, and sweatshirts. The space was lined with a half-dozen computers for people to post their reviews.

3. **Got the review while the experience is fresh and positive**

   DVDs of each individual tour are offered for sale and most families purchased a copy. It took about forty-five minutes to duplicate the DVDs and people had nothing to do, so many folks posted reviews while they were still ecstatic from their glorious adventure. Smart timing!

Blue Hawaiian Helicopters knows how to create trust using tech and, in the process, produces raving, supersatisfied fans!

Customers Never Think of Unsubscribing!

Online cycling store Nashbar is relentless with the pursuit of trustology. They know your buying patterns well and regularly email you with options and incentives. In a recent preweekend email, there was 70 percent off on more than one hundred select items. As a customer, you never even think about going somewhere else or *unsubscribing* because there is too much value at stake. Here's just a sampling of their retention strategy:

Forever Guarantee

At Nashbar, their guarantee says it all:

We believe in each and every one of the 10,000+ products we sell— from the most modest of cable ends to complete dream bikes—and we stand behind them 100 percent.

That means if for any reason you are not satisfied, simply return the item and we'll replace it or provide a refund. No muss, no fuss, no time limits.

That's right—we're talking forever. It's our promise to you and it's the best in the business.

Price Protection

Nashbar also promises to provide the lowest price on everything they sell. That means if you happen to find a lower price on a new, identical item (exact size, color, and model), they will match it.

Their Price Protection pledge doesn't end there! If a consumer finds a lower price for the exact product, even thirty days after his or her purchase, they will still match that price.

Live Experts

Have a question about an item? Nashbar provides the best technical support in the biz. Their crack crew of cycling experts are only a toll-free phone call, live chat, or email away.

Digital Valet

At the downtown Summerlin shopping center in Las Vegas, Nevada, there are no more valet tickets. Instead, the valet asks for your mobile number, enters it into a tablet, and asks for your first name and taps submit. While standing there, he or she confirms you received your ticket and the message along with it that says, "To request your car, click here." It is completely automated. When you are ready to leave and request your car by tapping the Request Car icon, you get an instant confirmation message. The final automated message you receive is the ticket to reclaim the car with these embedded instructions: "Please show this page to the valet." Not surprisingly, when we picked up the car, the valet smiled and asked, "How was your valet experience?" What would you have rated it?

Use these examples to build TRUSTOLOGY at your company. Make sure you make an impact at every level and give every customer a reason to KEEP COMING BACK.

ARCHITECTING PURPOSE

★ ★ ★ ★ ★

Chapter 3

True sales success doesn't begin with the stuff on the outside—whom you persuaded last week, how much you sold last month, what you earned last year, or how much you can afford to buy this year. Lasting success is built with the stuff on the inside—who you are and who you want to become, why you sell, and what legacy you intend to leave.

—TODD DUNCAN, *HIGH TRUST SELLING*

THE LAW OF THE ICEBERG: THE TRUEST MEASURE OF YOUR SUCCESS IS INVISIBLE TO YOUR CLIENTS

The only part of an iceberg you ever really see is the top. What you don't see is what's below the surface: the mass that supports the tip. The same is true for a successful company. What the customer doesn't see is what's below the surface; they only experience the top, the product, the service. The Law of the Iceberg creates a laser focus for an organization and its team. It gets everyone committed to a common cause and radically impacts the velocity of value they create in the marketplace, thus earning high ratings. It ignites a purposeful reason for being, attracting success and propelling significance through achievement beyond the realm of possibility! All of this is below the surface: the inside stuff, the heart and soul of the organization, the purpose for which it exists. If that's right, then the outside stuff like product, customer interaction, and yes, ratings, go through the roof.

Companies that thrive in the 5-Star world architect a purposeful reason for being. They promise something the customer truly values that creates impact on a very personal level. Today, a company must have a centering mechanism that gets and keeps everyone focused on impacting the customer in deep and meaningful ways. The more successful it is, the stickier the customer will be to the brand and the faster the brand will grow.

> *The highest use of capital is not to make more money,*
> *but to make money do more for the betterment of life.*
> —HENRY FORD

Ford's quote is the foundation for *5 Stars*. It's about bettering the life of a customer through product and service perception and performance. The deeper the connection, the deeper and more committed a customer is to the brand.

SoulCycle

What is SoulCycle? SoulCycle is an indoor cycling studio reinvented. At SoulCycle, they believe that fitness can be joyful. With inspirational instructors, candlelight, epic spaces, and rocking music, riders can let loose, clear their heads, and empower themselves with strength that lasts beyond the studio walls. On your bike, you climb, you jog, you sprint, you dance, you set your intention, and you break through boundaries. It's a community of sorts, each individual there for a reason more profound and important than "just another workout." **SoulCycle doesn't just change bodies; it changes lives.**

AT SOULCYCLE...
WE ASPIRE TO INSPIRE.
WE INHALE INTENTION AND EXHALE EXPECTATIONS.
WE COMMIT TO OUR CLIMBS
AND FIND FREEDOM IN YOUR SPRINTS.
WE ARE A FITNESS COMMUNITY
RAISING THE ROOF AT YOUR OWN CARDIO PARTY
THE RHYTHM PUSHES US HARDER
THAN WE EVER THOUGHT POSSIBLE
OUR OWN STRENGTH SURPRISES US EVERY TIME.
ADDICTED OBSESSED,
UNNATURALLY ATTACHED TO YOUR BIKES.
HIGH ON SWEAT AND THE HUM OF THE WHEELS.
CORE ENGAGED, WE RESHAPE OUR ENTIRE BODIES,
ONE RIDE AT A TIME.
CHANGE YOUR BODY
TAKE YOUR JOURNEY
FIND YOUR SOUL.

On our first visit we noticed an entire wall in the studio with SoulCycle's passion and purpose painted on it! During the session, the instructor constantly used words and phrases from this list of motivating, life-altering expressions, affecting the mood of every rider.

We felt every bit of this as we wiped off the sweat and headed home having had a 5-Star experience.

Purposeful Change

In her article, "How Great Companies Think Differently," organizational change expert Rosabeth Moss Kanter says this about "Iceberg Thinking":

> Institutional logic holds that companies are more than instruments for generating money; they are also vehicles for accomplishing societal purposes and for providing meaningful livelihoods for those who work in them. According to this school of thought, the value that a company creates should be measured not just in terms of short-term profits or paychecks but also in terms of how it sustains the conditions that allow it to flourish over time. These corporate leaders deliver more than just financial returns; they also build enduring institutions.

Great companies create frameworks that use societal value and human values as decision-making criteria. Companies believe that corporations have a purpose and meet stakeholders' needs in many ways: by producing goods and services that improve the lives of users; by providing jobs and enhancing workers' quality of life; by developing a strong network of suppliers and business partners; and by ensuring financial viability, which provides resources for improvements, innovations, and returns to investors.

Purpose is the pivot point that allows a company to foundationally decide the impact it is going to make in the lives of its employees and customers. Purpose also allows a company to bet the success of the firm on a strategy, creating indelible and repeatable moments of magic in customers' lives. Companies like Apple, Patagonia, TOMS, LinkedIn, REI, PG&E, IBM, Cisco, Zappos, and Verizon Wireless to name a few all have a purposeful focal point on why they each exist, and it sets the stage for a 5-Star experience.

If you and your organization want to have a high impact on the customers you serve and create a 5-Star experience for them as often as you can, a great exercise to begin with is completing this checklist:

The Law of the Iceberg Checklist

☐ What does our picture of success look like?

☐ Why are we in business?

☐ What do we want our brand to be known for?

☐ How does what we do matter?

☐ Where are we going?

☐ What will guide us?

☐ What difference are we going to make?

☐ How will our customer be transformed?

☐ How will we be remembered?

THE GREAT AMBUSH

★ ★ ★ ★ ★

Chapter 4

> *Cell phones, mobile email, and all the other cool and slick gadgets can cause massive losses in our creative output and overall productivity.*
>
> — ROBIN SHARMA

Technology has snuck up on business. We knew it was coming but most of us had no idea the impact it would have on us. The truth is we've been ambushed. Employees actually only work 60 percent or less of their scheduled work time. There is a difference between being busy and being productive. Companies today that win the ratings race must have a culture of focused productivity where every individual pursues the highest levels of efficiency by taming technology and boosting achievement. *Productive, engaged employees are more likely to create happy customers, which lead to higher ratings.*

Rapid advances in technology, paired with globalization and fast growth, combined to rewrite the rules of success, failure, and organizational design and structures. A little over twenty-five years ago, we had no mobile phones, no Internet, no email, and no cable news channels. For the first time ever, there are more gadgets in the world than there are people. According to GSMA Intelligence, the number of active mobile devices and human beings crossed over somewhere around the 7.19 billion mark. It's good, or maybe it's bad, or maybe it's ugly.

The purpose of understanding the ambush is not to challenge the obvious; that technology is here to stay. Rather, it is to understand that technology is neutral. It can be used for the betterment of the customer experience, and it can also distract from that betterment. Email can be good, or it can be bad. Texting can be good, or it can be bad. Social networking can be good, or it can be bad. Whatever level you are at in the organization, you must impress upon people what is at stake, and then you must lead the charge to employee efficiency. If you don't, whatever role they play, they will create drag in producing the overall best customer experience, and thus ratings.

Ambushed by Email

A Harris Poll showed that the average working professional spends about 23 percent of the day emailing, checking it an average of thirty-six times per hour. The expectations placed on employees have now encroached on their nonwork time, time used to recharge and rejuvenate at some serious levels. According to an article by Dave Gilson

- **22 percent** are expected to respond to work email when they're not at work;
- **50 percent** check work email on the weekends;
- **46 percent** check work email on sick days; and
- **34 percent** check work email while on vacation.

Inspired by these statistics, Gloria Mark of the University of California, Irvine, and her colleague Stephen Voida, infiltrated an office, cut thirteen employees off from email for five days, strapped heart monitors to their chests, and tracked their computer use. Not surprisingly, the employees were less stressed when cut off from email. They focused on one task for longer periods of time and switched screens less often, thereby minimizing multitasking. The professors had the following conclusion: "Our study has shown that there are benefits to not being continually connected by email. Without email, our informants focused longer on their tasks, multitasked less, and had lower stress."

There is a gold mine here. It's called momentum. Going back and forth between tasks reduces overall effectiveness during the day, potentially impacting a client experience.

Ambushed by Socializing

Here are some statistics to consider: According to a CreditDonkey.com survey, employees spend an average of 7.6 hours per week on social media on the job with 70.4 percent of social media users admitting they visit the sites only for personal purposes. Bolt Insurance calculated that visiting nonwork-related websites such as Facebook, Google+, Twitter, and Pinterest creates a financial drain of $130 billion from employees not performing work-related tasks. This is a lot of time that could be spent improving and impacting customers and their ratings.

Ambushed by Texting

The average adult spends a total of twenty-three hours a week texting. There are more than six billion text messages sent each day in the United States alone. Worldwide, sixteen million text messages are sent per minute. It is the number one use of mobile devices; therefore it is not surprising that it is also a top interrupter of productivity. While texting is gaining traction in sales, marketing, and service efforts, it still ranks as one of the top reasons employee workflow is compromised.

Ambushed by Interruptions

Focus precedes success. Interruptions destroy the momentum that focus creates. Stop the interruptions, and you improve the productivity. Don't, and you take more time than necessary to complete other, often more important, tasks and initiatives. Improve productivity and you're likely to improve the customer experience. For example, *TIME* magazine reported that on a typical day, workers are interrupted seven times an hour, which adds up to fifty-six interruptions a day, 80 percent of which are considered trivial.

7X
an hour

56
interruptions

80%
trivial

Ambushed by Meetings

Researchers led by University of North Carolina at Charlotte's Steven Rogelberg found that unproductive meetings cost U.S. businesses $37 billion a year. And when employees are in meetings, they are often not focused. According to a survey conducted by FuzeBox, a video conferencing platform, 92 percent of people say they multitask during meetings. Meetings need to be short, focused, and have a call to action with accountability or they are a waste of time.

Ambushed by Multitasking

Multitasking is a weakness! According to *Psychology Today*, in a study of more than five hundred full-time workers, Harvard University reported that constant multitasking increases the time it takes to complete a task by as much as 50 percent.

Have your ever tried this? While you are on a conference call, you are writing up a sales report, checking your email, and texting your friend about hitting the bar after work. You think that is multitasking. IT'S NOT!

It's task switching, not multitasking—the term *multitasking* is actually a misnomer. People can't actually do more than one task at a time. Instead we switch tasks. So the term used in research is *task switching*. And task switching is expensive. You make more errors when you switch than when you do one task at a time. If these tasks are complex, time and error penalties increase.

Every part of being ambushed impacts the aggregate outcome a company and employees deliver to the customer, directly or indirectly. Solve this puzzle and attaining 5 Stars is the prize.

5-STAR MOVES FOR TAMING TECHNOLOGY

There is nothing wrong with technology. Business needs it. But there is everything wrong when technology is not managed, especially in the area of employee productivity. The idea here is if the employee is more productive, it should impact the happiness of customers at some level, and thus the ratings those customers give to the brand. Here are five moves that will give the customer a better experience due to employees using effective time management:

5-Star Move No. 1: Batching

The most successful methodology to tame the technology interruption is batching. Handle all things technology related during preordained time slots, and when you are done, turn the technology off until your next slot. Start with more frequent blocks of time for email, texts, and voicemails. Then, as you get more proficient, move to less frequent blocks of time. Having 9:00 a.m., 11:00 a.m., 1:00 p.m., 3:00 p.m., and 4:30 p.m. slots for fifteen minutes will allow you to get more done and not lose productivity to constant starts and stops.

5-Star Move No. 2: The Cone of Silence

Silence is golden. As we wrote this book, we were off the digital grid. There is nothing more important than this task, right here, right now. We use out-of-office replies to let people know and promote this book:

> Thank you for your message. Today is a writing day. Our next book is *5 Stars: Building High Ratings and High Trust in the Digital Age* and will be released next year. Thank you for your patience and we will respond the next business day.
>
> Our phones are off. Email is off on all machines when we are writing. What we are doing is the most important thing we should be doing; **nothing** should interrupt it.

You will improve your speed of execution and get a higher quality result.

5-Star Move No. 3: The 5-Minute Rule

Philip Dormer Stanhope, the Earl of Chesterfield, said, "Take care of the minutes, for the hours will take care of themselves."

If insanity is doing the same thing over and over and expecting a different result, then this rule will give you sanity. It's very simple. Every sixty minutes, take five minutes and evaluate the previous fifty-five minutes. Were you productive? Did anything take you off course? Are there repeat offenders that zap your time? Reset your course for the next hour and commit to staying more on track. Getting the most important things done gives you mojo, improves your self-esteem, and enhances productivity.

5-Star Move No. 4: Jamming

Focused thinking, aka *jamming*, is putting the most important thing you focus on during a limited time into a confined space. Jamming is forced productivity, becoming hyperfocused on a single task for a blocked period of time. You can designate the time frame but it's recommended that a "jam" session be at least sixty minutes and no longer than ninety minutes before you switch back to batching. Examples include sales, service calls, research, client follow-up, brainstorming, etc. These experiences should be at least two to three jam sessions per eight-hour day for optimal output.

5-Star Move No. 5: Delegation in the Digital Age

Successful entrepreneurs, businesses, and teams realize that the tug-of-war between doing what they are good at and all the other things that need to get done is only solved through efficiencies and delegating those tasks to other people. This model allows everyone in the organization to do what they do best, resulting in improved performance and engagement—all of which are necessary in the digital age to impact the customer experience. In the past, the limitation to full-blown delegation has always been head count, fixed cost, and justification. That has all changed with the introduction of the virtual assistant.

With companies like Zirtual, Red Butler, Fancy Hands, Ruby Receptionists, or EA Help, anyone can delegate "virtually" anything without the hassle of hiring a full-time assistant. Virtual assistants can schedule meetings, manage your calendar, book travel, respond to emails, and complete other business tasks. They can pay bills, order gifts, deal with customer service, schedule doctor's appointments, and more. The list of what these companies can do is endless and well worth the money if you want to optimize your and your team's productivity without hassle. Remember, do what you do best and delegate the rest.

Don't be ambushed—tame the technology dragon. A happy employee creates happier customers earning higher ratings.

"The Internet has turned what used to be a controlled, one-way message into a real-time dialogue with millions."

—DANIELLE SACKS

STORY
SELLING

★ ★ ★ ★ ★

Chapter 5

> *The brands that win are the brands that tell a great story.*
>
> — MITCH JOEL

In Hollywood, the storytelling capital of the universe, the pitch is everything. Success or failure rests on one's ability to tell a story in a sentence or two. If you can't pitch your idea, no one will buy.

Businesses need pitches. Products need pitches. Salespeople need pitches. We call it story*selling*—selling through a memorable and easily repeatable story that has indelible impact. A great, compelling story wins more stars when it come to ratings.

Story*selling* is particularly critical in our high-trust, high-tech world. People long for human connection. Meaningful stories create emotional bonds with prospects, employees, investors, vendors, clients, and

What's your story?

even products. Stories help people remember who you are and make it easy to retell and then sell what's unique about you to others.

Good companies are story*sellers*. Your company's origin story has great power. Regardless of whether your company started in a garage, a dorm room, or some far-off land, there is a story behind it. People want to be part of something bigger than them. They want to be a part of story with a happy ending.

There is an award-winning print and design company called Moo in the United Kingdom. They are passionate about great design and the difference it can make in people's lives. On their website, they story*sell* by asking you a question: **"What would the most beautiful business**

card in the world look like?" Questions can be a part of story*selling*. One great question and customers can create their own stories about your company and product.

When we wanted to have the most beautiful business cards in the world, Moo delivered! Every time we give out our cards, people rave they're the coolest cards ever. We are story*selling* Moo.

Products need story*selling* and great stories don't need to be told, they can be shown. Sara Blakely had a product but no sales. She wrangled an appointment with a Neiman Marcus buyer in Dallas and arrived wearing a formfitting pair of white pants. Sara invited the buyer to the ladies room where she demonstrated the pants with and without Spanx and the product was on the shelf three weeks later. Today Sara is a billionaire.

Products can be the hero and save the day for someone who has a problem. For example, bike lights are not sexy or compelling. Salva Menn, cofounder of Fortified Bicycle Alliance, a manufacturer of heavy-duty, theft-resistant bicycle lights, knew this. He and his team struggled to come up with their story. After days of thinking about their angle, inspiration hit. "Our friend had his bike light stolen, and then he got hit by a car coming home." It's memorable, connects, and communicates the emotion of safety. Any person can retell it after hearing the story once, and it makes the primary selling point—*buy our light, save your life.*

Salespeople need to story*sell*. We were at a business seminar with two thousand people when Louise, an elegant Southern brunette, sauntered in wearing a beautifully tailored pencil skirt, a fitted jacket, pantyhose, and military combat boots. Louise is a mortgage banker from Louisiana with a passion to serve the military in her community and help them get into homes. If Louise walks into a room, you want to know her story, and you'll never forget it. P.S. We've never seen Louise without her combat boots on.

We love stories; we remember stories that move us, touch our hearts, or inspire us. Make your story prominent on your company website and tell it often.

THE STORYSELLING RECIPE

Hero:
1. Why did we launch the company?
2. What is our grand purpose?
3. What is the emotion we are trying to tap into?
4. Why are we committed and passionate about the opportunity?

Villain:
5. What problem needed to be solved?

Goal:
6. What is our unique factor? How are we different from the pack? What sets us apart? How's our philosophy superior to our competition?

Knowing People's Stories Matters

Steve Jobs started Apple in his garage; then he went up against the almighty Microsoft and won. J. K. Rowling was a divorced, unemployed, single mother on welfare. She had a dream to become a writer, and today she is richer than the queen of England. Mark Zuckerberg, along with some college roommates, started Facebook. Originally, a simple premise to use social networking for classmates to stay in touch, it now boasts over one billion active users a month. These are all modern-day heroes with compelling stories.

Emotions capture hearts and minds and determine our options and buying decisions. It's more psychological than logical, more unconscious than conscious. Customers want to be impacted positively, emotionally, and memorably during a sale. According to Gallup, businesses that optimize this connection outperform competitors by 26 percent in gross margin and 85 percent in sales growth.

Mankind has always relied on storytelling to record history and communicate. Businesses need to rely on story*selling* to create impact and make a difference. Connecting with people on both an intellectual and emotional level is powerful and will increase sales.

Seven Steps to Great Story*selling*

The important elements in story*selling* are:
1. Make it simple.
2. Make it short.
3. Make it easily repeatable.
4. Make it memorable.

Extra credit points if you also:
5. Make it emotional.
6. Make it include a grand promise.
7. Make it have a villain to overcome—your product or service has to solve something negative.

> *In a world where people have a lot of choices, the story may be the deciding factor.*
> —NICK MORGAN

VIDEO TELLS A STORY

Over the past two decades, we've come to rely more on the faceless communication tools of emails, text messages, and social media. Every day, we turn our most important messages over to the channels of communication that are most devoid of personality and clarity. This is not story*selling*. The weight-loss clinic mentioned in chapter one knew this and chose a unique route. During the most important phase of winning our trust, they used video several times to effectively communicate the impact of the program.

My friend Connor McCluskey, CEO of BombBomb Video Marketing, says this shift is critical in winning and keeping customers for life. Here's how he describes it:

> All your typed-out text is missing something critical—you! And an ever-growing set of emoticons can never overcome your absence from your communication.
>
> Are you better over the phone, or are you better in person? You're better in person. We all are. That's why we're in sales. If you can just get them to take the appointment, you'll connect and move this opportunity forward. Face, voice, personality, energy, interest, and expertise—it all comes through so much better in person.

As fellow human beings and as social creatures, we connect and communicate with each other so much more effectively when we're together in person. It's in the eye contact. It's in the nonverbal communication. Your business thrives on face-to-face connection, but there are two obstacles that get in the way.

The obstacles are the time and distance that prevent us from connecting with people in person as often as we can and should. People are too far apart or too busy to get together in the same place at the same time. Our lives and our businesses are less complete and satisfying as a consequence.

As you may have noticed, video is less expensive and more common than ever. And it's far more human than typed text. Through video, you can be there in person when you can't be there in person.

Instead of sending typed out messages that you're not very good at writing and your customers are not very excited about reading, you can send your face, voice, personality, expertise, and energy in channels you're already using—email, text, and social media.

It's like leaving a voice mail with your webcam, smartphone, or tablet. It's more personal and differentiating. It is far more clear, and it is much more emotional—fueling deeper connection.

Record and send messages when it's convenient for you. The people who receive them open them up and experience you when it's convenient for them. Have satisfied customers record V-monials to help others get comfortable with your product and service. Use video on special occasions and milestones in the customer life cycle.

Companies are adopting this all over the world and are building trust and humanizing their businesses by moving back to the face. Through simple video.

LOVE 'EM OR LOSE 'EM

Chapter 6

> *There is only one boss—the customer. And he can fire everybody in the company from the chairman on down, simply by spending his money somewhere else.*
>
> — SAM WALTON

The new mandate in the 5-Star world is to fall in love with your clients, really fall in love, and keep them coming back for life. If your clients are in love with you and your brand, they will never leave you and they will tell the world about you. If you don't love them, you *will* lose them, guaranteed.

The piece of high-trust selling that does the greatest good and has the highest impact, the humanity piece, is at risk of being pushed out by technology. Humanity is code for connecting, and we need to do a better job of making our customers feel special. Forrester Research revealed that 89 percent of consumers felt no personal connection to the brands they buy. Without that emotional bond, customers could be tempted to try a competitor's product. In the new world of selling, emotional attachment equals loyalty and increases the likelihood of earning 5 Stars.

EMOTIONAL COMPETENCY

Answer this question: What is the *emotional competency* of your organization? Tony Hsieh, CEO of the online mega shoe retailer Zappos, says this about the company and their commitment to emotional connection: "Every call is perceived as a way to make a positive emotional connection with the customer. Today's customer must be positively, emotionally, and memorably impacted at every level of his or her commercial experience, from start to finish." Emotional competency is caring, helping, and being genuinely interested and concerned for the customer beyond the transaction. It's about capturing hearts and minds.

It is simply putting the long-term relationship ahead of the immediacy of the sale. Both are important, but the reality is the former drives the latter, and that will never change.

According to an Ipsos MORI study, emotionally engaged customers

- are at least three times more likely to refer;
- are four times more likely to repurchase; and
- are 44 percent less likely to shop around.

TRANSFORM THE CUSTOMER

How will your customers be transformed by your product or service? No matter what you sell or why someone is buying what you have to sell, what are they really looking for? On some level, they're looking for transformation. The secret is not in the product or the service, but what it does for the buyer. *Logical business tactics* say the purpose of the customer is to get the sale. *Emotional business strategy* says the purpose of the sale is to get the customer and, because of the emotional connection, keep them for life.

We must be in love with the customer, not the product, pitch, message, or features. We must help instead of promote, focusing on what customers want, not what we want. We need to pull rather than push the customer into a relationship with our brand. We must talk less and listen more. We must serve, not sell, and give more than we ask. Sales are made because of who you are, not by what you say. We must make fewer statements and ask more questions. Depending on your product or service and whether the interaction is face-to-face or a tech solution like embedded chat windows, when customers are online, everyone needs to know key discovery questions that pull the customer into a relationship with the brand.

Storyselling questions include:

- ☐ What's important to you about this product?
- ☐ What are you trying to achieve with this resource?
- ☐ What look are you going for with this outfit?
- ☐ What are your most important goals with this software?
- ☐ What could we do to serve you better?

These types of questions flip the script. Look at the approach Apple took in its ads. Instead of features and benefits and gadgetry, the ad said, "We believe in changing the status quo and thinking differently. We build beautifully designed tools that unleash your creative potential and help you change the world… Want to buy?"

Your transformational message must have a higher purpose backed by vision; it must sell dreams, not features, benefits, and cost. You need to see your business as a vehicle to help others enhance their lives.

Set up transformative experiences and increase the odds for 5 Stars.

> *A question is the most powerful force in the world.*
> —TODD DUNCAN

THE LAW OF INCUBATION

Incubation is the DNA for profitable customer relationships and must exist in all phases of the client life cycle. The goal is to create conditions that promote, transfer, or add more value while growing loyalty, and repeat and referral business exponentially. We call the three most critical areas to create and deploy value *Love Zones*:

1. Acquiring new customers
2. Optimizing customers' purchases and service experiences
3. Retaining and cultivating customers for repeat and referral business

These zones are where we fall in love and stay in love with our clients. Master these and you lock out the competition and incentivize customers who will buy from you and promote you forever.

THE THREE LOVE ZONES

Love Zone No. 1: Acquiring New Customers

Every business needs customers. Acquisition is the front end of business success, and like the combination to a lock, this is the first number. You've got to have it. It's important.

You can offer rebates, incentive programs, special offers, coupons, promo codes, giveaways, or special events. You can buy lead lists, make cold calls, send direct marketing, send catalogs, send print mail, and purchase old-fashioned advertising, but all pale in comparison with power of the consumer experience and their subsequent referrals and reviews.

The key to lead generation and acquisition is to drive your lead cost down to the lowest level possible while simultaneously driving conversion to the highest level possible. In this new world of selling, product performance and customer ratings with a real-time customer connection are what will keep you on the leading edge. The least-expensive marketing is when you have hundreds, perhaps thousands or even millions, of people telling the world about you and your product and your company because of their experiences. It's called **earned advertising** and is the most powerful acquisition tool there is.

Who Is Your Dream Client?

Getting more business is rarely found by getting more clients. It's found by having more valuable clients. Because you can't be everything to everyone, or you will fail at being the right thing to the right one, we recommend having half the clients and give them twice the value.

Companies and salespeople have heard it a million times, but they rarely follow the 80/20 rule. The rule states that 20 percent of your customers produce 80 percent of your sales. But that's true only if you focus 80 percent of your time and service and marketing efforts to that group. Instead, most allow the 80 percent of customers who only present 20 percent of the business to consume 80 percent of the company's time and resources. It's where most of the headaches, complaints, drama, and defection occur. And it's not because the product or service is necessarily bad. It's because that is the nature of the rule. The company that earns the highest trust and ratings knows how to leverage the rule through one simple idea—going deep.

The company uses technology and data to constantly narrow and filter in order to get to a smaller population of customers who can have the greatest impact on the business and ensuing referrals and reviews. It masters segmentation of a key target group—**dream clients**—who are highly influential people who can affect more than one referral, sometimes thousands. With social media, blogging, video, audio, and print testimonials, it is this group that can make the biggest dent in your lead generation effectiveness and ultimately your bottom line.

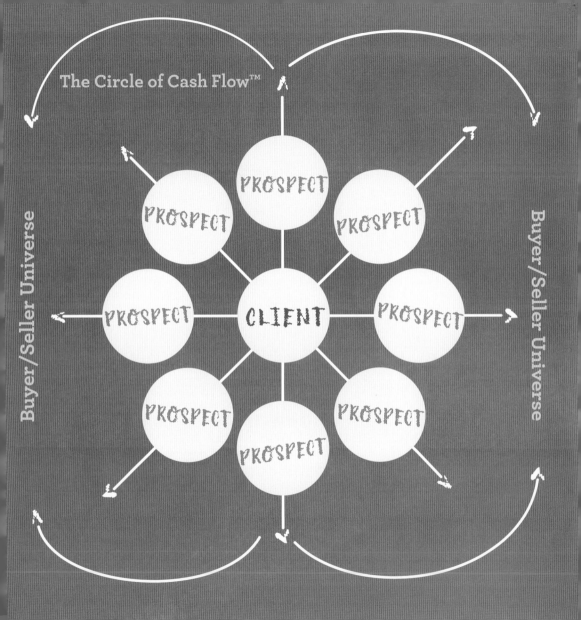

The biggest catalyst any company or salesperson can use to accelerate their leads, referrals, and ultimately business is based on the following premise: **the best sales and marketing are when someone who already knows, loves, and trusts you introduces you to someone you need to know.**

For example, five happy customers each tell eight people about your product or service. You now have forty new prospects checking your ratings and reviews. If those forty use you, and they have the same experience as the first five, you now have 320 potential clients. If the 320 use you and have the same experience, you now have 2,560 potential clients. This one model applies to almost every business model you can think of. Existing customers know the customers you and your business need to know.

If you kick this idea into high gear, instead of one person telling eight, one person could tell eighty, eight hundred, or even eight thousand. It's your gateway to the buyer universe.

A mortgage broker we know caught the vision of this as a small business owner. Instead of prospecting one potential home buyer at a time, she asked the key question: *Who do I know who knows who I need to know?* Within two months, she was referred to the HR director for a 17,000-employee business, for which she is now the primary lender. Her business has gone up 800 percent in six months. Why talk to one hundred leads to get one sale when you can talk to one lead and get one hundred sales?

The lowest-cost lead with the highest potential to convert will always be the one-to-one *referral.*

One-to-one referrals

- ☐ cost little to nothing to acquire;
- ☐ trust you faster;
- ☐ decide on you more quickly;
- ☐ negotiate less;

- shop other options less;
- are lower maintenance;
- are interested in loyalty;
- repurchase more often;
- refer you more regularly; and
- eliminate the need for costly ineffective marketing.

WOM
=
Word of Mouth

WOM Rules

The best form of advertising is advocacy. In a study by Zendesk, an overwhelming 90 percent of respondents claimed that positive online reviews motivated their buying decisions. A whopping 86 percent said buying decisions were negatively influenced by reviews that weren't positive.

Millennials rank WOM as the number one influencer in their purchasing decisions about clothes, packaged goods, big-ticket items (like travel and electronics), and financial products. Baby Boomers also ranked WOM first as the marketing influencer in their purchasing decisions about big-ticket items and financial products, and they ranked it as the third-highest influencer on their decisions to buy packaged goods.

And there is more:

65% of new business comes from WOM referrals (*New York Times*).

65% of respondents trusted WOM referrals from people they knew (*Nielsen*).

> *Customers acquired through WOM add two times the lifetime value of customers acquired through traditional marketing. Customers acquired through WOM spread more WOM and bring in twice as many new customers.*
>
> —MICHAEL TRUSOV, RANDOLPH E. BUCKLIN, AND KOEN PAUWELS, "EFFECTS OF WORD-OF-MOUTH VERSUS TRADITIONAL MARKETING: FINDINGS FROM AN INTERNET SOCIAL NETWORKING SITE"

Love Zone No. 2: Optimizing the Customers' Purchase and Service Experiences

> *We value a unique product more than just the commodity. We value convenience more than a unique product. We value a unique experience more than we value convenience.*
>
> —B. JOSEPH PINE II AND JAMES H. GILMORE
> "THE EXPERIENCE ECONOMY"

This is the most important part of the three Love Zones. It's the second number of the combination. It is where the magic takes place and the stars are earned. And it must be carefully choreographed and executed flawlessly to make the lasting, indelible impact it needs to. Everything rises and falls on the customer's experience, period.

If businesses knew the true lifetime value of a customer, they would make different decisions in executing a strategy to optimize their experience. Sadly, the stats are in and the amount of defection from brands where customers don't feel loved is staggering. Here are some results from the Zendesk survey:

66% of B2B and 52 percent of B2C customers stopped making purchases after a bad experience.

95% of respondents who have had a bad experience told someone about it or posted negative reviews.

If we are going to love our clients, we must know why and what we love about them, what they love us for, what their disappointments are with other vendors and suppliers, and what their expectations with us are. That simple formula sets any company and salesperson up for success. The number one 5-Star rule is *Don't Break Their Hearts*. You must positively deliver every time. Here's a personal experience that drives the point home.

The $6,000 Egg

How much would you pay for an egg? Fifty cents? Two dollars? How about $6,000?

That's how much it cost one restaurant in Newport Beach in lost business when they refused to honor our simple request.

We were frequent patrons at a chic test kitchen that experiments with new menu items. One day, the featured special was a waffle served with an egg on top. We wanted a cheeseburger, which was on the menu, but we asked to have a fried egg added on top of the burger. We were totally surprised to hear from the server that the kitchen might not be able to do that. Even though they were making eggs for the waffles, the server told us the kitchen was too busy to make one for our burger. So we asked a different server who also knew us.

The answer was still no, because it wasn't on the menu. When we asked to speak to the manager, she approached without a smile. After yet another request, she stood firm, explaining the restaurant only orders a

certain number of eggs per day, and they couldn't sacrifice one for our cheeseburger.

We were really confused. Where was the love? We asked her, "So a one-time visitor who orders a waffle for fifteen dollars is more important to you than a $6,000-customer who comes in at least four to six times a month?"

Her response was a textbook lesson in terrible customer service. "If we run out of eggs, we can't serve the waffle." When we suggested she might be able to send a busboy down the block to buy a few extra eggs, she offered to cover our check for our inconvenience.

We couldn't believe she would rather pay our seventy-five dollar tab than sell us a single egg. We left and vowed never to return.

We wound up at Whole Foods next door where we shared our experience. There, the server told us that their company creed is "We don't say no here." And they don't need the manager's permission to satisfy customer requests. We custom ordered something. No hassle. Smiles and "Yes, we can." We had an incredible experience and moved our money and our loyalty to a new restaurant that loves us. 5 Stars in action.

Love Zone No. 3: Retaining and Cultivating Customers for Repeat and Referral Business

> *Marketing is actually what other people are saying about you.*
> —SETH GODIN

Retention is the mother lode. This is the third number in the combination. It's the asset that produces the most profitable cash flow a business can have. And, sadly, too many business and salespeople in today's fast-paced world of business ignore it. In the last twelve months, we have transacted with thirty-one different brands. After our purchases, we only heard from five of them as a form of keeping us engaged, which set us up for the next repeat purchase, referral, or both.

The business that values their customers will create followership on purpose. They never assume they will get the customer to come back, realizing that out of sight is out of mind. They believe in the Law of Response that states, **"If we don't follow up with them, they won't follow through with us."**

If they want their customers for life, they have to connect with them during their lives, giving them a reason, an incentive, a purpose to come back time and time again. And they realize they have to do all this with a ton of love, courting, wooing, and swooping customers off their feet time and time again.

One of the most powerful examples of strategic retention is Harley-Davidson. They don't want satisfied customers. Their aim is to find, nurture, and develop loyalists. They have created a following of nonconformists. Rarely does one construct a brand that has equal amounts of cultural significance and product association. You would think that a rough-and-tumble brand like Harley-Davidson would not care about aggressive optimization. Nothing could be further from the truth.

Harley-Davidson does not just sell motorcycles. The company has applied the Law of the Iceberg. It has architected passion and purpose into its existence. What Harley-Davidson offers you are the keys to becoming an untethered badass. Every employee knows it and feels a sense of pride behind the brand, as well as a sense of inherent dedication. One of its coolest retention strategies is their calendar of events. These include dealer events, barbecues, bike shows, tours, rides, rallies, and more. Within an hour of where we live, there are more than forty-five events in the next thirty days. And they are *always* packed!

Do or Die

Retention is an afterthought for a lot of companies and their associates. Everyone thinks about increasing brand impressions and launching new products. That's good, and it is necessary. But even more important is the strategy on how to support and nurture the preexisting audience.

As much as we want new customers, remember that when it's all said and done, you're nothing without the people who made you what you are. Most companies see new followers and subscribers as the key to success. From a sales and marketing perspective, there is no greater need, then, to understand the preexisting base is a hundred, or even a thousand, times more important and valuable.

THE
NEW
HANDSHAKE

Chapter 7

> *I have no contracts with my clients;*
> *just a handshake is enough.*
>
> —IRVING "SWIFTY" LAZAR

Before this virtual, high-tech world, it used to be that the handshake was the first impression. You met someone, sized them up, and upon greeting them, you made eye contact and locked hands in a firm handshake.

Strangers formed impressions based on the grip of the hands, posture, energy in the voice, and maintaining eye contact. Was the handshake limp? Who looked away first? What was the opening sentence?

Those days are gone. In today's world the "handshake" takes place long before two people meet. People want to know *who* they are going to meet. LinkedIn; Facebook; Google; your company bio, website, and profile photo *are* your new handshake. Does your virtual presence communicate the story you want to tell or story*sell*?

Recently, we hired a virtual assistant. The company emailed the assistant's social link so we could get to know her before first contact.

What was likely endearing to her friends was a turnoff in a business relationship. We didn't hire her. Next! We chose another virtual assistant over this gal, and she never knew it. There are no second chances. There are too many options, and that deadly first impression is nearly impossible to undo.

You will be judged and vetted by potential clients before you ever meet.

The handshake means a lot. Always has and always will. In the world of trust and ratings, it is more important than ever. The handshake, whether virtual or physical, still signifies acceptance between the seller and the buyer. However, before the final handshake ever happens, the seller must make a powerful, positive, and persuasive first impression, or the buyer is gone.

Out of a thousand real estate agents, we chose one who had a compelling promise on his website, used V-monials from satisfied customers, and sent a personal video thanking us for viewing his site. We met and looked at homes, but we were running out of time for him to show us all the properties we wanted to see. Without blinking an eye, he put us up in a luxury condo overnight, covered the change fees on our flights, and sold us a home the next day. We've introduced him to hundreds of people.

What about an elegant restaurant that has a dress code prohibiting shorts? Instead of turning us away, a restaurant staff member escorted Todd to a private closet that had loaner pants. A couple of hours later, we paid our two-hundred-dollar tab. The next day, the restaurant sent a thank-you text. A week later, they sent a text message to come back and provided an incentive. We returned to the restaurant nine times in the next year.

These examples have one thing in common: from start to finish, these businesspeople built trust, used technology, delivered service, and thrilled us. And it started with a virtual handshake.

The stats are in and in the high-trust, high-tech world, you have only seconds to make the first handshake. Then, throughout the transaction, you must keep shaking hands to optimize and keep the customer forever.

No. 1: Nail the First Impression—*Quickly*

The window to make a strong first impression with a customer continues to shrink. In a study published in *Psychological Science*, Princeton psychologists Janine Willis and Alexander Todorov reveal that it takes only a tenth of a second to form an impression of someone when you first meet. Two additional studies give us a whopping seven seconds.

At best, you've got only a few seconds to accomplish this initial step in optimizing your customer's experience.

Additional research shows that 90 percent of lost sales are due to curt emails, typos, poor grammar, poor personal hygiene, the visual look and feel of print and website, and the tone of voice used in a voicemail or in a phone conversation.

Perfect the welcome. Start strong. Research from the University of Glasgow Association for Psychological Science and Graduate Recruitment Bureau shows the importance of nonverbal cues. For instance, they have four times the impact of verbal ones. In face-to-face situations, it's best to wear professional attire and work on projecting good posture, a positive attitude, friendly eye contact, a firm handshake, a smile, and a look of confidence. Then practice four steps of the verbal part of your welcome: introduce yourself, name-drop a reference or other client, make a statement of impact, and ask a question focused on providing uniqueness and value. Here's an example: "Hi, I'm Jenny. It's a pleasure to meet you. I'm grateful Tom asked us to meet. I look forward to working with you to reduce the time between your clients' calls for repairs and when your service team arrives on-site."

Roll out creative, VIP treatment as part of your welcome too. We know of a company that enhances first impressions by having customized welcome signs reserving the best parking spots for client visits. Another one shows tailor-made welcome videos for new clients to begin their first meetings. Another simply offers a printed beverage menu so special visitors have more options than coffee or water. Another has V-monials playing in the lobby while clients wait for their appointments.

Do your homework. You need real connections to develop lasting relationships with your customers. Start by learning about them via LinkedIn, Google, Facebook, and even the customers' own web pages. You'll arm yourself with their photographs and knowledge of their businesses, circles, hobbies, music, and special interests. All of your contacts have topics they love to discuss, and it's smart to have an idea of what the likely connection points are. These connections move prospects and new clients to a higher level of trust and appreciation, lowering their resistance to doing business with you.

No. 2: Go Big with Service or Go Home

Favorable impressions that are not backed by strong performances are worthless. Defaqto, an independent researcher of financial products, and Harris Interactive reported that 86 percent of consumers would pay more for a better service experience. Only 7 percent of U.S. consumers say that customer-service experiences they have with companies typically exceed their expectations, according to the Echo Global Customer Service Barometer. Forrester Research revealed that 45 percent of consumers abandon online transactions if their questions or concerns are not addressed quickly. According to the RightNow Customer Experience Impact Report, 89 percent of consumers have stopped doing business with a company after experiencing poor customer service.

No. 3: Make Milestones Matter

Transactional milestones are any events that move the customer through the purchasing experience. Regular communication during a transaction answers customers' questions before they are asked, gives them peace of mind, and secures the success of the transaction and the relationship.

For example, online party supply retailer Shindigz lets you know the status of your order every step of the way, and the company celebrates you throughout the process. Here's one of five emails we received on one order. Talk about using high tech to create high trust.

Dear Deb and Todd (aka Shindigz Customers of the Day),

CONGRATULATIONS! You are now our new most favorite customer! If we were with you right now, we would definitely give you a high five. As of this moment, your order is currently cruising along the virtual highway and stopping at the best party supply company in the world!

You will receive another awesome and highly entertaining email from us as soon as your items ship.

Talk about a hook!

Relationship milestones are events or interests in your customers' lives. What if you called every customer on his or her birthday? We program our smartphones with reminders for our top clients' and friends' birthdays and click "alert" so we don't forget. We take the end date for these calls to their hundredth birthday. Currently, we make more than seven hundred phone calls a year to clients on their birthdays. BaBaam! **High trust, high tech, high touch.** Technology at its best. By the way, don't send email birthday messages—too tech and not enough connect. Instead, send an anniversary card every year on the date of the customer's first order with you.

Bottom line—if you are not in touch with your clients, you are out of touch.

No. 4: Keep Them Coming Back

Over the years, we have purchased steaks as gifts for key clients from ten suppliers that never did anything to land a second sale. But two years ago, we sent fifty clients a Christmas gift from Chicago Steaks. In the November following that purchase, Chicago Steaks sent us a summary of our previous order that let us simply check a box if we wanted to send a gift to that client again. The document listed every client along with a mailing address, the gift the client received last year, and the holiday message included with that gift. Wow! Chicago Steaks made our lives easy, a key to keeping customers coming back.

No. 5: Nail the Last Impression!

Survey your customers regularly during any transaction. Great waiters do this repeatedly during a meal. A dentist does this during a procedure. Smart businesses do it constantly during and after a transaction and, if they are smart, for the life of the customer. If there are any problems, they can be addressed sooner rather than later. You have to finish every transaction strong, forming an indelible impression that sets the stage for the next order, purchase, or referral. Then, use video to say thanks! After every speech, we send a thirty-second video from the car on the way to the airport. The meeting planner forwards it to all attendees.

Big business or small, you must finish strong!

"If your business is not on the Internet, then your business will be out of business."

—BILL GATES

BUSINESS AS UNUSUAL

Chapter 8

> *One customer, well taken care of, could be more valuable than $10,000 worth of advertising.*
>
> —JIM ROHN

Business is changing at a faster pace than ever. Consumers are more educated, their expectations are higher, they have more choices, and your competitors are better than ever. If your service is not at *level ten*, you will lose sales, revenue, and, if you are not careful, your company, or your job. World-class service is not the future! It's here now, and if you are not on board, you will lose!

The key to having a successful 5-Star company rests in the Law of the Encore that states **the greater the performance, the louder the applause.** When your applause goes up, that is code from the customers that they want more—more of you, your company, your products, and your services.

One for One

In 2006, online retailer TOMS released the documentary *For Tomorrow*, which showcases the company's mission to donate a pair of shoes to a child in need for every pair a customer purchases. Then AT&T used TOMS in a commercial showcasing how the company uses AT&T technology to stay connected to the world. The rest is history—TOMS reached thousands of customers who then used their social media platforms to tell the rest of the world about TOMS.

TOMS innovated the one-for-one giving model: buy a pair of shoes and TOMS will donate another pair to someone in need. They provide real value with a huge social and economic impact. The company applied its business model to eyeglasses in 2011 and then began selling coffee and donating clean water to the coffee-growing communities. Since

2006, TOMS has given more than fifteen million pairs of new shoes to children in need and helped restore good sight to more than 250,000 people. It has more than one hundred *giving partners* in more than seventy countries, focusing on how best to integrate shoes into larger community development programs in health, education, and well-being.

TOMS is also innovative in connecting with its passionate base of customers to create customers for life. It's different from traditional marketing because they're not just a shoe company. They're not just selling—they've created a movement. Their content is about the impact they and their customers want to make in the world. It's not about the shoe—it's about making a difference.

What's A Buffer?

Buffer is an app, and it is the best way to drive traffic, increase fan engagement, and save time on social media. It's simple. Add updates to your Buffer queue and they will be posted for you spaced out over the day—and at the best times. Drop your tweets, Facebook stories, or LinkedIn updates in and you don't have to worry about when they will be posted; it's all taken care of by Buffer for you.

Buffer loves their customers in an unusual way. Leo Widrich, the cofounder of Buffer, describes the priority his company places on customer happiness in a blog post by Help Scout's Gregory Ciotti:

> *Starting with "why" is absolutely important. Giving the best customer support possible is at the very top of our list. It is the **number one thing** we want to get done every day. That's also the reason why we call our support team a Happiness Team.*

This is especially commendable for a highly social app that supports an intimidating amount of free users in addition to its paid clientele.

You have to ask: Why would the Buffer team place so much emphasis on support if they have a ton of free users already?

According to Leo:

> Instead of us going out and telling everyone how amazing Buffer is, which is much less effective, we want to do it in a different way. We let people come to us with any problems or questions they have. We then help them in the fastest and best way we can and they go away feeling happy and WOWed telling their friends about us.

Leo shows how great service turns from, "something we should be doing" into a precise and **targeted** method of generating amazingly positive word-of-mouth referrals. When you look at all of the references that Buffer gets on major news sites and industry-leading tech blogs, it appears that this strategy is certainly working.

Being different and disruptive changes the game. Getting customers to say "wow" is about doing things differently than the rest of the market. Often by going above and beyond with big and little things, you can become the sole leader, ahead of the pack.

Happiness

IS A
TEAM

VALUE RULES

★ ★ ★ ★ ★

Chapter 9

> *Try not to become a person of success, but rather try to become a person of value.*
>
> —ALBERT EINSTEIN

Real, transformative value is simply the art and science of giving customers what they want, need, and desire and then backing it with a 5-Star experience that is second to none.

BREWING UP CHANGE

In 2009, after a dismal performance cut the company's stock in half, Starbucks looked to high tech to help reengage their customers. Adam Brotman was hired as the vice president of digital ventures. In one of his first moves, Starbucks offered Wi-Fi in all of its stores. That also included a digital landing page with a variety of digital media choices, including tons of free content. Brotman said, "We are not just doing something smart around Wi-Fi, but we are doing something innovative and valuable around how we were connecting with customers."

Brotman, now chief digital officer at Starbucks, teamed up with Chief Information Officer Curt Garner and formed a close working relationship, restructuring teams to collaborate about how to add the most value to the customer experience. For example, customers wanted shorter lines, so they cut ten seconds from every card or mobile phone transaction, reducing time-in-line by nine hundred thousand hours. In addition, they added mobile payment processing, processing more than eight million transactions a week, and rolled out a "just-in-time" mobile add-on so you can order from your mobile device and have your order waiting for you when you arrive. **The lesson: take care of the value and the sale happens.**

To create real and meaningful value for your customers, remember it's about people and people don't remember stuff. They remember experiences. Positive experiences aid in three key truths:

1. Customer cultivation must be strategic.
2. Advocates are far more valuable than advertisers.
3. The value of a business is in the strength and stickiness of its customers.

Adam Contos is the chief operating officer for RE/MAX, where he oversees one hundred thousand real estate agents, consistently equipping them to be effective. **"Value opens the door. The more value given, the wider the door gets,"** he said, which is significant for two reasons. First, at a tactical level in the organization, you need to understand that most companies think the purpose of the customer is to get a sale. Second, at a strategic level, the purpose of a sale is to get a customer. It's the latter that matters most.

Much, Much More from Much, Much Less

Getting more from less couldn't be more appropriate when it comes to high-trust selling in a high-tech world. But it's also not enough. **You must get much, much, much more from much, much, much less!** Here's an example of research from TrackMaven, a competitive intelligence firm for digital marketing:

In early 2014, just after the 2013 holiday shopping season had finished, the marketing team at U.S. retailer Pottery Barn had a clear objective: to make Pinterest an effective marketing channel for the company. With its corporate image and product set seemingly tailor-made for Pinterest, it seemed like a no-brainer to expand its presence there.

During the first few months of the year, it seemed that progress was being made. From January through July, the team quadrupled its monthly output of Pins from 38 to 170, though follower count increased only 11.4 percent, from 214,829 to 239,144. With closer examination, it became clear that trouble was brewing. Despite the modest follower growth, Pottery Barn's content was actually doing less and less for them.

While their Pinterest output quadrupled, Pottery Barn's engagement level (measured on Pinterest as the combination of likes, re-pins, and comments) was falling off a cliff. Their average interactions per pin decreased by nearly 75 percent, from a high of 402 in January to 109 in July. In the midst of summer, with the 2014 holiday season right around the corner, the Pottery Barn team found themselves facing a content marketer's nightmare: more content with less impact.

Their results paint a dark picture of content marketing, but the efforts also yielded some valuable insights for marketers looking to cut through the noise with their content-creation strategies.

Digital platforms appear to be doing more harm than good in the race to get and keep customers. With social networks, email, and blogs, there is a tendency to blast out as much content as possible in a "more is better" approach. Today's consumer is bombarded by content, but nothing is ctrl   alt   delete   getting through. Most marketing messages are not sticky, but rather act as Teflon, leaving the consumer in a "ctrl-alt-delete" frame of mind.

The best way to cut through all the noise is to produce valuable and meaningful content. This is especially critical in social media. For example, the TrackMaven study showed that more than 50 percent of all posts on Twitter, Pinterest, Google+, and LinkedIn receive fewer than ten interactions. Twitter had the lowest—73 percent of tweets receive less than ten interactions. Instagram had the highest with only 10 percent of photos and 6 percent of videos receiving less than ten interactions.

Here's the problem with the high-tech piece of value—marketers are getting better at distributing content, but they are not getting better at creating content that is worth distributing. It's not the volume but the value that matters most!

Pottery Barn 2.0

When more content wasn't working at the Pottery Barn, it was time for a shift, a pivot, a reboot. Call it what you want, but they went from ho-hum, run-of-the-mill content to rediscovering their purpose—reinventing content that went way beyond Pottery Barn to focus on helping their followers create better homes. Whether you bought from them or not, the messages could be used and therefore were *valued*. By October of the same year, and three months after a near disaster, Pottery Barn posted only sixty Pins and raked in 345 interactions. That was a 300 percent improvement in engagements with a decline in Pins of 110 percent.

THREE KEYS TO CREATING REAL VALUE

No. 1: Humanize Your Company

We had dinner with James Symond, the CEO of Aussie Home Loans, a very successful mortgage brokerage based in Australia. They have had unprecedented growth, providing more than $20 billion in home loans each year in a country with a population of only twenty-four million people. When we asked James what he thought the keys to the company's incredible success were, he said, "We brought humanity back into the transaction."

If you have ever gotten a mortgage, you probably know how overwhelming it can be. You become a "transaction" to the lender, complete with a loan number and a list of hundreds of pages of documentation that you have no idea what it says. James said, "We don't do transactions; we transform lives." His team "works harder than anyone else and we are constantly using technology to learn about our

competition and how to position Aussie as a better solution." The end result is a smooth, remarkable transaction with the right advice and the right product that meets the financial needs of the home buyer. They don't do loans; they impact families' lives for the better. "At the end of the day," says James, "we want them to think of us as their financial partner for their whole life when it comes to real estate." They don't do consultations over the phone or use Skype, Google, or Facetime; they do them face-to-face. They connect with the heart before they even speak to the head.

Humanizing your company will force you to think about your purpose and your core reason for being in business in the first place. It should transform the entire customer experience, and your customers should feel it.

Connection is the key. If you connect, you can convert. If you convert, you can close. If you close, you can cash in through repeat and referral business.

No. 2: Build Value That Sticks

The high-tech world is not actually creating more high trust. It's creating the opposite—less trust. According to TrackMaven, from 2013–2014 content output by companies increased by 78 percent, but engagement decreased by 60 percent. Nearly half of professionally marketed blog posts receive fewer than ten interactions. One in four receive zero! Obviously more *is not* better. Value is a quality game, not a quantity game. We live in an extremely noisy universe and there is too much content sent out for any of it to be readily and actively deciphered fast enough and with enough trust to yield higher levels of engagement, conversion, and ultimately business.

The goal is a loyal customer who loves you and your brand and whom you love. The characteristic of this type of loyalty are customers who

- make regular repeat purchases;

- ☐ purchase everything you sell that they could possibly use;
- ☐ encourage others to buy from you; and
- ☐ demonstrate immunity to the pull of your competitors.

Customers won't stick around unless you give them a reason. There are simply too many options and messages that don't matter. In this world, the words "sticky marketing" is all about making the customer return to your business time and time again by creating more and more value. We call it *brand lock-in*. It gets the customer to a place where they can't live without you.

For your brand to have the "stickiness effect," content should be:

- ▣ **Simple:** Keep it easy. Make messaging uncomplicated. Have a profound core message and make sure it comes across memorably.

- ▣ **Disruptive:** Messaging should be unconventional and disrupt the customer's conventional line of thinking, holding their attention.

- ▣ **Compelling:** Messaging should move people to action.

- ▣ **Emotional:** Stay away from logical deliverables like price, costs, and timelines. While important, the emotional connection trumps them almost every time. Include emotional triggers.

- **Narrative:** Stories sell. The more proof you use about how others have been impacted by your products and services, the more likely newer customers will migrate to you.
- **Consistent:** Build valuable content regularly and make sure it is current, relevant, and resourceful. This increases the shares, which is code for inexpensive lead acquisition and conversion.

No. 3: Make Sure Your Brand Has Emotional Attachment

Management guru Peter Drucker once said, "People buy with their hearts, not their minds." We think that simple thought defines the new 5-Star world better than any other. The competition is not for the customers' money; it is for their emotions.

A company's sales and service effort has to connect deeply. No matter your product or service costs, if there is no emotional attachment, the customer isn't as likely to stick around. Think of this concept as your *irresistible magnet*.

More than 70 percent of a purchase experience involves emotions on some level. Emotions shape the attitudes that drive decisions and behavior. They also impact behavior far more than technical, performance, and functional factors.

All buyers are influenced by their emotions. They just may not realize it. How customers care about your products and/or services may be unconscious, but these unconscious feelings can have a very concrete impact on your business. Emotional connections can determine the yes or no in buying.

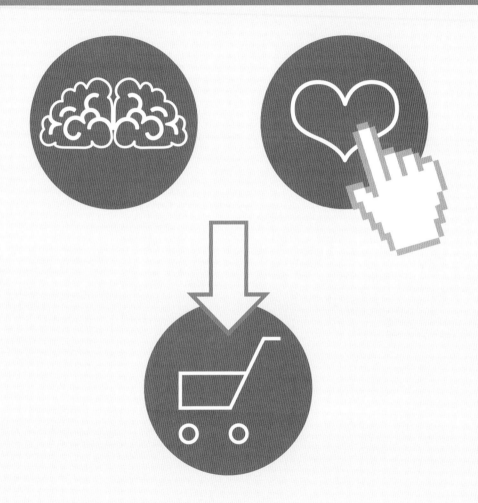

THE TRIPLE ~~THREAT~~ OPPORTUNITY

★ ★ ★ ★ ★

Chapter 10

> *Do unto others as they'd like done unto them.*
>
> —DR. TONY ALESSANDRA

Everyone buys differently. The need to segment sales and marketing efforts by generation is more pressing than ever. If you don't segment your selling efforts, you could miss up to two-thirds of the buying population and opportunity. The new mandate is you have to sell the way a generation wants be sold to. Don't pay attention to this truth and it's a *threat* to your survival. Pay attention to it and it's where the real *opportunity* lies. Customize your sales and marketing efforts to appeal to these unique generations and you can win big. Niche a generation and sell to them the right way and you can make a fortune.

How you say something is as important as *what* you say, but it's mandatory to know *who* you are saying it to. Different generations want to be sold in different ways; they have different life experiences and priorities.

BABY BOOMERS

There are approximately eighty million Baby Boomers in the United States. They have the highest disposable income of any generation, and they are living longer. Boomers are hard workers. Their parents or grandparents lived through the Great Depression and they were taught to value a dollar. They started with written-based knowledge: information came from newspapers and books; research was done at the library; letters were sent by snail mail. They contacted people by mail or telephone. Letters were typed on a typewriter or handwritten. The telephone was a landline and had to be answered; there was no answering machine or voice mail.

Receiving information electronically came from radios, until the black-and-white television was born, and eventually became a color television.

Families had one television located in the living room, with limited network channels and shows. They grew up on *The Mickey Mouse Club*, *The Ed Sullivan Show*, *I Love Lucy*, and Walter Cronkite reporting on *CBS Evening News*. To change the channel, someone had to stand up and walk over to the TV, so everyone watched commercials and no one channel surfed. (Boomers watch more television today than other generations and spend less time on other platforms.)

Many families shared one car, married couples had a closet the size of a door, families shared a bathroom, and vegetables came in a can. It was common for clothing to be sewn by mom or ordered out of a mail-order catalogue; it was a treat to drive to a store. They are the generation most likely to use a coupon and are still likely to want paper receipts or statements. They use cash to pay for things or paper checks.

Boomers are the first divorced generation, yet they are nostalgic about traditions, family, country, and their religions. They are more concerned about saving the neighborhood than saving the world. They want high touch, not high tech—they want a phone call, not a text or email. Letters, especially hand-written, are appreciated.

Boomers want to be sold face-to-face and don't care what a bunch of strangers they don't know say about a product or service. They want facts and appreciate information. Don't rush them; time is not of the essence. They are the least likely to purchase online; a little photo of a product and descriptive blurb isn't satisfying. They'd rather drive to a brick-and-mortar store, see a display, have a salesman ask questions, read the salesman's body language, and pick up a product and touch it. You win them with the right words and sincerity. How you say things is as important as what you say.

- Do court them: it makes them feel good, hip, smart, sexy, and hungry.
- Do ask great questions, then "show and tell": high trust, high touch.

- Do write hand-written notes and keep communication personal and respectful.
- Do listen closely, and stay focused in the conversation to advance relationship.
- Do call them on the phone and use social proof. Ninety-six percent of them participate in word-of-mouth marketing.
- Don't create overly busy website designs: their use of technology is on the rise, with 75 percent using it, but they demand simplicity.
- Don't pressure or talk down to them, as they have the money and the options to go somewhere else.
- Don't think of them as old: they want to stay and look young and have the money to spend to make that happen.

Generation X

They were exposed to technology early and are more comfortable with it than previous generations. Gen Xers saw the tech evolution bring forth microwaves, fax machines, call waiting, answering machines, voice mail, computers, and the Internet. Telephones became cordless and cell phones morphed into mobile devices that text, search the Web, record video and voice, email, take photos, and play games.

Cash was replaced with ATM cards and bills are paid online. They witnessed the technology paradox—they are more connected to others and yet more disconnected.

Garages got bigger; individual family members have their own cars. TVs hang in many rooms including bedrooms, bathrooms, even in the kitchen. The Disney Channel broadcasts twenty-four hours a day and mouse ears can be purchased online. The invention of the remote control birthed channel surfing, and hundreds of programs were available. Walk-in closets became prevalent and designer brands affordable. Gen Xers care more about labels and brands than other generations. They innately understand that the world is full of many options.

Families had two incomes and more disposable income. Kids spent less time with their parents, and the cost of housing went up significantly. The divorce rate skyrocketed and first marriages became an anomaly. Anyone can purchase web domains, start a blog, business, or website. Individuals found their voices and an audience. Facebook exploded; people counted their "friends." The world got smaller.

In 1968, the Apollo 8 crew left Earth's orbit for the moon and took the first color photograph in which the entire planet was in full view. When the picture was published, the entire global population had a shift in consciousness. The beauty inspired a green movement focusing on caring about the environment. Paper was replaced by eBooks and electronic newspapers and magazines, and self-publishing became

141

possible. Alternative energy sources, hybrid cars, and solar panels become options. Fresh food, organically grown vegetables, sustainable restaurants, and health became a priority.

Xers have money and a desire to shop, spending reportedly $128 billion a year. They have lived through the bubbles and bursts; they're natural skeptics, a consequence of growing up in the information age. They're not distrustful, but they will have an issue if your offer is all sizzle with no substance. They are content-centric.

Xers like individual offers, so they feel unique and special. They appreciate the value of a good deal, but you don't need to slash prices. Instead, explain the value of your offering in honest terms. They must feel comfortable with a salesperson before they are comfortable with a product. You can build rapport with a physical presence; they like looking eye-to-eye to judge things.

Xers are not afraid to try new things. Give them a reason to try your product or service.

- Do make it tangible and show how the product or service impacts their lives.
- Do focus on improving their financial security when possible.
- Do engage digitally: TV, print, and radio are their media spots.
- Do stick with the facts, especially if the facts can save them time.
- Do use before-and-after sales analogies.
- Don't use nostalgic images in advertising; use real people. They love being reminded of their childhoods.
- Don't use hype or pitches but focus on benefits: 80 percent of this group is actively engaged in social media.

- ▣ Don't give long-winded presentations or waste their time.
- ▣ Don't slash prices. Increase value and talk about how it impacts them.

Millennials

Millennials were born with mobile devices in their hands. Digital is their norm. They take selfies and have received lots of trophies. Their universe is global, and they live in an always-on digital world that is paperless. They live online and purchase online.

They are used to instant access, information at their fingertips, and producing results quickly. Everything is interactive and immediate: texts, Skype, FaceTime, Google+, chat rooms, Snapchat, Instagram, YouTube, and blogs. They are excellent at self-promotion, highly social, and exceptional influencers.

They have lower employment rates than other generations, less income, and more debt. Millennials are putting off milestones like marriage, children, living independently, and buying homes, but have not entered their peak home-buying years. Some are moving home after college, unlike previous generations. The trend will be multigenerational living, with grandparents, parents, and adult children living under one roof.

They are the generation least likely to buy luxury goods and more interested in the ability to use an item than to own it. They are willing to share a home, a car, or any other big-ticket item. Author and economist Jeremy Rifkin predicts, "Twenty-five years from now, car sharing will be the norm, and car ownership an anomaly."

They are the largest of the three generations and collectively the most passionate about living green, repurposing, recycling, and sustainability. They buy brands that embody their values and make them feel good about themselves. Health is a priority. They eat smarter, exercise more, and are more willing to spend money on wellness.

Millennials are plugged into one platform or another eighteen hours a day. The only time they are not on a technology platform is when they are sleeping. Mobile devices made shopping easy for them, and 50 percent of purchases are on their phones, so buying is a click away.

To reach them, optimize your sales, marketing, and website for the best mobile experience possible. They are most uncomfortable—borderline anxious—without their phones. Estimates are that a millennial is exposed to a thousand advertisements a day. Mobile marketing is key.

Don't market to them on television, direct mail, or through telemarketing, and whatever you do, make your message an *emotional story*. It will more likely be shared on social media.

Remember they were raised on sound bites; make your point and then shut up. They were born busy, so you have to make your sale quickly, in two minutes or less. You must speak their language and at their speed. Vine videos are six seconds. In fact, in the last two years, Vine, Snapchat, Viadeo, and Soundcloud have in excess of 715,000,000 active monthly users.

They're more price sensitive and less interested in the brand. Brands are shrinking in importance. Quality and having a social cause makes them more loyal to a brand than price. When purchasing, they're highly influenced by peers and social media. Ratings and reviews help make their purchase decision.

The message and the messenger must feel authentic. Realize you will be fact-checked with multiple sources almost before you have finished. The worst thing you can do is try and sneak something past them.

They are more narcissistic. The individual comes first—50 percent of their purchases are based on emotion. Emotions drive this generation and it's more psychological than logical. These consumers want to be positively, emotionally, and memorably impacted during a sale. When you connect to their hearts, they are three times more likely to recommend you and repurchase from you, and they are 40 percent less likely to shop around.

- Do make things on demand.
- Do create a mobile-friendly, digital experience for them.
- Do advertise your social impact: How you are changing the world?
- Do help them show off how unique they are.
- Do market with SMS—texting wins.
- Don't sell them what they don't need.
- Don't market to them in print. TV is where half learn about a product.

- ☐ Don't call them unless it's important, and if it is—text.
- ☐ Don't try and be cool to relate to them.
- ☐ Don't expect them to drive to your store.

SUMMING IT UP

Never before has there been such a diverse population for businesses to serve. The purchase power is amazing. In order to optimize all this opportunity, companies either need to tailor their marketing and messaging, or be very focused on key niches they want and can serve brilliantly.

If you are an individual sales professional, you must tailor your message and be aware of how you are influencing each group. If you sell to them the way they want to be sold to, your conversion rates and sales go up. So does repeat and referral business.

THE FUTURE HAS ARRIVED

> *Ten years from now you will surely arrive. The question is: Where?*
>
> — JIM ROHN

We are standing at the edge of a moment in history. To leverage our success, we can take what was great about the past and bring it into the future. This is an exciting time to be alive. We cannot begin to imagine the technological advances we will see in our lifetimes.

As our homes and offices fill with cutting-edge technology, our humanity is going to become more important and must be protected. We believe our humanity and ability to connect will be the bridge between us and our clients' hearts.

Business has never been about dollars and cents. It is, and will always be, about people and relationships. Your customer will never leave you if you add value that they cannot get anywhere else. Create happy customers. Generate repeat business. Receive massive referrals. Support this with brilliant service and technology experiences that make customers feel great. Commit to earning 5 Stars! You will thrive!

YOU are the future. The future is HERE!

ACKNOWLEDGMENTS

We would like to thank David Paley for the research contribution he made to this book. David is a graduate of Vanguard University, and we predict he's going to tear it up in the business world. We would also like to thank our executive assistant, Alicia Barata, who manages our lives and made it possible to have the time to devote to a book of which we are significantly proud. To the most amazing parents in the history of the world, Hal and Connie Morris and Grant and Gloria Duncan, who collectively have been married for 106 years. Your character, strength, faith, and love inspire us every day!

Thank You!

Deb Duncan is president of American Television Ventures. She has been a pioneer in the direct-response television industry. Starting in college, she was a producer of *Everybody's Money Matters* on the Lifetime Television Network. She has written, produced, and directed more than one hundred direct-response TV programs. She has great insights on how to frame your message and how to get people to respond.

Deb is the author of two children's fairy tales, *A Thousand Princes* and *Mrs. Prince*, as well as several screenplays.

For more than twenty years, **Todd Duncan** has earned a transformative reputation worldwide as a top trainer, motivator, and personal coach for business professionals in the sales, mortgage, real estate, and financial services industries. Todd's influence in the peak-performance world impacts more than 250,000 people annually around the globe, and he has personally coached some of the world's top-producing sales professionals.

Todd is the author sixteen books, including the *New York Times* bestsellers *Time Traps: Proven Strategies for Swamped Salespeople* and *High Trust Selling: Make More Money in Less Time with Less Stress*. His books are in forty-four languages with more than one million copies in print.

Todd has been featured in the *New York Times*, the *Wall Street Journal*, the *Los Angeles Times*, the *Seattle Times*, *Entrepreneur* magazine, and *SUCCESS* magazine, and on the Success Network, *The Dave Ramsey Show*, and FOX News, among other media outlets.

As leading experts in the field of High Trust Selling™ and service training and development, Deb and Todd provide real solutions to the challenges businesses face in the new world of commerce.

To explore having them speak at your next corporate meeting or training, or to inquire about additional services, contact Alicia Barata at alicia.barata@toddduncan.com.

Together, they authored

The $6,000 Egg: The 10 New Rules

of Customer Service, which changes

the way companies engage customers

uniquely and blow the doors off

service as usual. It is available at

www.theduncangroup.com.

Books by Todd Duncan

available at SimpleTruths.com

TODD DUNCAN

SALES
MOTIVATION

GREAT QUOTES TO FUEL YOUR PAS

TODD DUNCAN

The Simple Truths of
SELLING

Lemonade
50¢

The Most Important Things You Should Know

THE $6,000 EGG

Customers are lost as a result of an unsolved service breakdown, and they will share their stories with everyone.

This book is about not just good service, not just great service, but exceptional, off-the-charts service. The kind that doesn't just WOW customers—it blows their minds.

The rules have changed. Today, the options customers have to get what they want are so plentiful that not a single company, or representative of that company, can afford to be powerless in the competitive world of service.

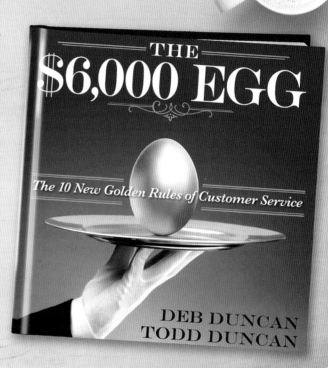